Summary of

Good to Great

Why Some Companies Make the Leap...And Others Don't

by Jim Collins

Instaread

Please Note

This is key takeaways, analysis & review.

Copyright © 2015 by Instaread. All rights reserved worldwide. No part of this publication may be reproduced or transmitted in any form without the prior written consent of the publisher.

Limit of Liability/Disclaimer of Warranty: The publisher and author make no representations or warranties with respect to the accuracy or completeness of these contents and disclaim all warranties such as warranties of fitness for a particular purpose. The author or publisher is not liable for any damages whatsoever. The fact that an individual or organization is referred to in this document as a citation or source of information does not imply that the author or publisher endorses the information that the individual or organization provided. This concise summary is unofficial and is not authorized, approved, licensed, or endorsed by the original book's author or publisher.

Table of Contents

Overview

What does it take to make something—an activity, a work of art, a company—great? What are the factors that distinguish the merely good from the truly great? In *Good to Great: Why Some Companies Make the Leap...And Others Don't*, Jim Collins offers insight into what makes a business truly great.

As the adage goes, "good" can be an enemy of "great": it can stop us from striving for more. It keeps us satisfied and content with something that is above average but not outstanding. In the business world, some companies are great from their inception; most companies, however, have to work hard to get to "good." Only some will ever reach greatness. Others get stuck in the good category, unable to make that final breakthrough that sets the few apart from the majority. *Good to Great* offers a way to understand what the distinguishing factors are between the companies that make it to "great" and the companies that do not. Findings are based on a comparative study between companies that made the move from good to great and sustained great results for at least 15 years and companies that failed to make the leap or, if they did, failed to sustain it.

With interviews from executives, empirical data, qualitative and quantitative analysis, and more, it becomes possible to explain what accounts for the difference between good and great companies. There are seven key principles to which great companies adhere across the board; by comparison, companies that failed to become great were notable for the ways in which they did not adhere to these principles. Any organization can dramatically improve its performance if it applies the principles of companies that have transformed themselves from good to great.

Important People

James C. "Jim" Collins, III: A graduate of Stanford Graduate School of Business, Collins is a business consultant and bestselling author who frequently lectures about leadership and building strong companies. He contributes to publications such as *Harvard Business Review* and *Fortune* and is the author or coauthor of six books, including *Built to Last: Successful Habits of Visionary Companies* (1994) and *How the Mighty Fall: And Why Some Companies Never Give In* (2009).

Darwin E. Smith: Smith was the CEO of Kimberly-Clark for 20 years, beginning in 1971. He turned a below average company into a great company.

Colman Mockler: Mockler was the CEO of Gillette from 1975-1991. Collins uses Mockler's remarkable stewardship of the company as an example throughout the book.

David Maxwell: Maxwell was the CEO of Fannie Mae from 1981-1991. By Collins's estimation, Maxwell practiced exemplary leadership.

F. Ken Iverson: Iverson was the CEO of Nucor from 1967-1998, transitioning it from a good to great company.

Alan Wurtzel: Wurtzel was the CEO of Circuit City from 1972-1986. Collins regularly uses Circuit City's transformation into a great company as an example to highlight his principles.

Joseph F. Cullman, III: Cullman was the CEO of Philip Morris (1957-1978).

Charles R. "Cork" Walgreen, III: Walgreen was CEO of Walgreens from 1971-1998. He had the vision to focus on the changing needs of the consumer and structured the company's strategies accordingly, transforming it into a great company.

Carl Reichardt: Reichardt was the CEO of Wells Fargo from 1983-1994, transitioning it into a great company by focusing on hiring the right people.

Lee Iacocca: Iacocca is a superstar former Chrysler CEO whose leadership style was driven by his dynamic personality. Collins argues this is why the success at Chrysler did not endure after Iacocca's departure.

Key Takeaways

1. Great leaders combine tremendous personal humility with unwavering professional resolve. They are not focused on personal gains but on setting up the whole company for success.
2. Hiring the right people for a company is the most important first step to greatness. Before deciding the "what" of strategy, vision, and organization, it is important to decide the "who" by identifying the people who will help execute major decisions.
3. Companies that are trying to become great must force themselves to confront brutal facts and difficult realities in order to address them. At the same time, however, they must maintain belief that they can prevail in becoming great.
4. A company must be best at its core competency to become great. This means understanding what the company is truly best at doing—not just what it wants to be best at or thinks it should be best at—and sticking to this competency consistently.
5. Going from good to great requires a culture of discipline. This does not mean having a leader who disciplines employees harshly, but hiring

people who are self-disciplined and committed to focusing their energy on the company's core competency.

6. Technology neither makes a company great nor makes it fail. Rather, great companies use technology as a way to accelerate momentum in line with their core competency.
7. The transformation from good to great does not come in a dramatic swoop or sudden action. It is a long process that requires persistent effort.
8. These principles are timeless and they apply even in a rapidly changing business world. Economies are always evolving and even if the present challenges look different from past ones, the principles for reaching greatness remain the same.

We hope you're enjoying this
Instaread book
Download the Instaread mobile app to get unlimited text & audio summaries of bestselling books.

Visit instaread.co
to learn more.

Analysis

Key Takeaway 1

Great leaders combine tremendous personal humility with unwavering professional resolve. They are not focused on personal gains but on setting up the whole company for success.

Analysis

There is a tendency to idolize larger-than-life celebrity CEOs and business heroes, but Collins's research team found that companies that prioritize hiring well-known leaders are actually not the ones that successfully make the leap from good to great. In fact, the leaders of companies that do make that leap are often people no one has ever heard of. They are not caught up in their own egos, riches, reputations, or future career moves. Instead, they tend to be humble, self-effacing people who are, at the same time, extremely driven to see their companies soar—and to see them soar even after leadership passes on to someone else.

If the underlying motivation for why a person wants to lead the company is difficult to ascertain, it may be difficult for businesses discern the leaders who have great ideas but ultimately seek personal gain from leaders who want to put the company first. This is why great CEOs often rise from within the companies they eventually lead. Shareholders unfamiliar with the company or its employees might ardently desire to see a famously successful CEO take the helm of the business in which they have invested, but such leaders are not reliable predictors of long-term health.

Lee Iacocca is an example of one such leader in the automotive industry. In recent decades, the tech industry has produced a number of high-profile leaders: Bill Gates, Mark Zuckerberg, and Marissa Mayer are admired and closely watched business leaders. But their success is owed to their knowledge of and focus on their core competency. None of these people would necessarily make a great CEO for a grocery company.

Key Takeaway 2

Hiring the right people for a company is the most important first step to greatness. Before deciding the "what" of strategy, vision, and organization, it is important to decide the "who" by identifying the people who will help execute major decisions.

Analysis

The adage "people are your most important asset" is flawed. In fact, it should state that the *right* people are your most important asset. Companies are only as good as the people who work for them. The companies that are good but not great tend to have a great leader who relied on good followers and helpers. But to be great, companies need to have great people in all positions, not just the leadership roles.

The distinction between "people are your most important asset" and "the right people are your most important asset" may at first appear to be insignificant. It seems obvious that the first statement assumes people are important assets so long as they are the right people for the job.

Nevertheless, expending the necessary effort to hire the right employees at all levels of operation is not something that every company does. Sometimes a company is so bloated and its mission so unclear that it allows its lower ranks to quickly turn over, or it fills them by relying on staffing firms that do not adequately understand the company's core competency or vision. This is sometimes the case even when these lower-level workers are the most visible or apparent part of the company, as with fast-food restaurant workers or customer support staff for telecom companies.

The emphasis on finding the right people at all levels dovetails with the first principle about leaders who are humble rather than egotistical: a great organization cannot just be about its superhero leader, especially since the leader cannot oversee the minutiae of the company's everyday activity, including recruiting and hiring. These two principles thus go hand-in-hand, and it is useful to see them in conjunction: a great leader knows that the company is not all about her, and so she takes great care to hire the right people for the right positions, so that she can trust them to hire the right people, too.

Key Takeaway 3

Companies that are trying to become great must force themselves to confront brutal facts and difficult realities in order to address them. At the same time, however, they must maintain belief that they can prevail in becoming great.

Analysis

Collins calls the act of striking a balance between these two different visions the Stockdale Paradox, after Vice Admiral James Stockdale, who famously endured four years of solitary confinement as a prisoner of war in North Vietnam. A company cannot get better unless it is honest about its problems and weaknesses. At the same time, and despite recognition of these problems, a company must sustain the faith that it is able to achieve greatness if it addresses its weaknesses honestly and adequately.

History has borne out this piece of wisdom many times. It is a historical commonplace that regimes will fail if they stop addressing internal problems that plague the state and its people in order to focus on new conquests. Tyrants and dictators characteristically surround themselves with sycophants who repeat only what they want to hear. The character Polonius, an adviser to the king in Shakespeare's *Hamlet*, is a satire of this well-known trope. The gratification offered by yes-men might be pleasing to a leader in the short term, but it is a disastrous strategy in the long term. It prevents leaders from confronting the facts, however unpleasant they may seem and however challenging they may be to overcome. Eventually, such leaders cannot sustain the illusions they try to perpetuate: people rise up against them, internal economic or political weaknesses damage them, or external weaknesses threaten them from without. This is one of the reasons that modern democracies value transparency in government: in theory, this effort to root out corruption holds leaders accountable, and the state as a whole is much stronger.

The same principle applies to business: honesty is the only way to square with the facts and have a chance at solving problems. Believing in an individual's or a company's ability to become better is also necessary to the process; it offers hope, optimism, and the motivation to implement positive changes. Still, it is difficult to be honest about shortcomings in one's conduct or business affairs. By emphasizing the need for "brutal" honesty and self critique in business, Collins acknowledges this difficulty while maintaining that although it is often painful to be honest with oneself, and easier to avoid reckoning with weaknesses, such honesty is still worth the trouble. Great leaders must overcome the innate desire to see themselves always in a positive light.

Key Takeaway 4

A company must be best at its core competency to become great. This means understanding what the company is truly best at doing—not just what it wants to be best at or thinks it should be best at—and sticking to this competency consistently.

Analysis

Companies have a tendency to stick with the thing that they have been doing for years or the thing for which they are most well known. But this is not necessarily the thing that a company is best at doing. To become great, companies must focus on their core competency.

This key principle intersects significantly with the key principle about confronting the facts and being brutally, unrelentingly honest. Businesses, like people, can easily be sidetracked by trends, fashions, and idealized self-perceptions. During adolescence, for instance, it is tempting to want to pursue an activity that is trendy or admired. The same applies to business, where certain methods or technologies come in and out of vogue. It is also tempting to pursue an idealized notion of one's strengths that is not necessarily consistent with reality.

Being honest about understanding one's core competency requires a kind of dedicated pursuit of self-knowledge for people and businesses alike. It may seem foolish for a business to discard an identity or activity with which it has long been associated. But if this identity or activity does not align with its present-day strengths and weaknesses, then it must be discarded in favor of a more honest assessment.

Notably, companies that failed to make the transformation from good to great tend to have their hands in too many different enterprises or projects. They lack consistency and are unable to focus on a single, overarching competency. This may seem like an obvious mistake, but it is one that occurs frequently in other life contexts. For example, children commonly pursue a wide range of extracurricular activities—soccer, dance, music, theater, and so forth—but anyone who wants to become serious and achieve excellence has to focus consistently on one thing. Sometimes it may seem prudent to diversify or explore other options. This, however, is not the path to greatness. Pulitzer

Prize-winning writers become great because they pursue writing, Olympic swimmers because they pursue swimming, and so on.

Key Takeaway 5

Going from good to great requires a culture of discipline. This does not mean having a leader who disciplines employees harshly, but hiring people who are self-disciplined and committed to focusing their energy on the company's core competency.

Analysis

With disciplined, competent employees, there is less need for bureaucracy and less need to find ways to motivate and incentivize behavior. The right people are self-motivated and self-disciplined to focus on the company's core competency and disregard other avenues. This does not mean they lack freedom or creativity, however. A culture of discipline fosters focus along with freedom and entrepreneurship.

This principle strongly recalls and expands on the earlier principle about making sure a company hires the right people. These people must self-disciplined. In part, this means they are motivated by the work the company does and are responsible, independent workers; thus, they do not need to be disciplined by external forces, such as a rewards system or a hovering manager. If a company's focus is paper products, for instance, then it needs to hire people who understand this core competency or who have the discipline to learn and to teach themselves everything they can about the paper business and its supply chain.

But self-discipline also refers to their ability to detach themselves from unnecessary activities and avoid needless competition within the company. This principle must also be reinforced at every level in the company. Great companies hire employees who are capable of eliminating extraneous projects and investing themselves fully in the areas where they can best help the company succeed.

Key Takeaway 6

Technology neither makes a company great nor makes it fail. Rather, great companies use technology as a way to accelerate momentum in line with their core competency.

Analysis

How a company responds to changes in technology is an important indicator of its ability to become great. The best companies are pioneers in using certain technologies, but they do not rely on technology to create their transformation from good to great. Lesser companies, by contrast, are afraid to be left behind by technological innovation and are less careful in their application of new technologies. Becoming great requires thoughtful use of insights about how a technology can align with a company's strengths.

This principle is really about avoiding the dangerous allure of chasing trends; in the twenty-first century, those trends tend to involve the latest gadgetry or disruptive new app. However, if a company abides by the previous principle about knowing and remaining focused on its core competency, then it will be better equipped to understand which technologies can accelerate and build on its strengths and which technologies might be distracting or even, in the long run, damaging to the company's success.

Innovation in the twenty-first century might appear to be more dependent on technology than ever before. Indeed, health care, transportation, finance, data analysis, dating, and so many other industries increasingly use and rely on digital and Internet technologies. Yet while individual technological inventions are often lucrative for their inventors, far more innovation occurs when companies or industries determine how they will respond to new technology. This is a crucial distinction. Savvy use of technology requires returning to the notion of self-knowledge and remaining focused on the company's best area of performance, even if that area is not part of the hot conversations in Silicon Valley or featured on the front cover of major tech and business magazines.

Key Takeaway 7

The transformation from good to great does not come in a dramatic swoop or sudden action. It is a long process that requires persistent effort.

Analysis

Going from good to great is not something that happens overnight—it does not happen with a single push or breakthrough or new acquisition. A sudden revolution does not provide sustainable, deep, or lasting change. Rather, the transformation to greatness requires patient effort in a carefully considered direction over the long term.

Edmund Burke, the conservative English political philosopher, wrote about the dangers and seductions of revolutionary thinking in his book *Reflections on the Revolution in France* (1790). His focus was not business transformation but political revolution in France. Yet his insights might be applied to instances of sudden, dramatic change across the political and business spectrum. Even before the worst of the bloodshed and terror had engulfed Paris and surrounding areas, Burke anticipated that such sudden transformation would be deeply destabilizing. For change to be safe, sustainable, and enduring, Burke believed that it needed to be implemented gradually and patiently, with due consideration given to all possible repercussions. [1] The Jacobins in France, by contrast, tore down centuries-old institutions in a matter of months and tried to erect totally new social, religious, and political processes that did not provide the basis for a stable society. [2]

Burke's insights and reflections resonate strongly with the recommendation that businesses should not attempt to leap from good to great with a single dramatic action. The eagerness to get to the end goal, whether it be a great company or a new political order, can itself prevent successful transformation by forcing the outcome too soon and too fast. Lasting change requires patience and persistence, not flashy, dramatic upheaval.

Key Takeaway 8

These principles are timeless and they apply even in a rapidly changing business world. Economies are always evolving and even if the present challenges look different from past ones, the principles for reaching greatness remain the same.

Analysis

There is a tendency for each new generation to believe it is confronting unprecedented challenges and change. This might be true in the specific contexts. But change is always taking place and there is always something new with which to contend. Principles for achieving greatness in business, however, are unchanging, and Collins describes them as being as immutable as the laws of physics.

Although businesspeople complain that the problems they face are unprecedented, or that the economy is changing faster than it ever has in the past, these basic principles for how to build a great business still apply. Even so, humans create business contexts, market regulations, and economic systems, which do and can change. Within modern capitalist systems, these principles for achieving great businesses may be invulnerable. However, “brutal honesty” about a business’s strengths may require acknowledging that contexts can and do change—sometimes in a fell swoop—and that businesses must account for shifting contexts as they evaluate their strengths and core competencies.

Author's Style

Though Collins's work is grounded in substantial research, analysis, and quantitative studies, he writes in a straightforward style, making his business principles understandable for readers with all levels of business background. He incorporates empirical evidence, including graphs, charts, and other data, to support his findings. But he also relies frequently on storytelling and factual anecdotes about specific companies and leaders in order to convey important concepts. Since many of the principles in this book are very general and abstract ideas about how companies should operate, the specific stories and concrete examples are useful for demonstrating the principles of greatness. They bring these abstract ideas to life, make them more comprehensible, and, most importantly, make them memorable for the reader who wants to adopt these principles in their own work.

Collins outlines the path from good to great in relation to seven key ideas embraced by companies that make this transition. He devotes a chapter to each idea, unpacking it and elaborating on it with an array of findings and explanations. This structure of dividing the key points into clear, distinct chapters makes his argument and principles easy to follow. Throughout his discussion of ideas, Collins refers frequently to his research process in order to shed light on how his team came to these principles and why they believe they are so important to understanding greatness. Collins maintains a tone of contrariness and thinking against the grain throughout the book: he repeatedly emphasizes that certain discoveries are surprising and that certain principles are unexpected and not necessarily conventional wisdom. Thus, *Good to Great* is a book interested in dispelling myths and misunderstandings about great companies in order to get to the truth about what makes a company great.

Author's Perspective

Collins is motivated to understand greatness and what distinguishes things that are average or "good enough" from things that are truly great. Though his focus is on understanding greatness in business, it is the overarching principle of achieving greatness, in any aspect of life, that he finds compelling. The idea for this book—understanding how greatness happens in order to achieve it—came from a fellow businessman who pointed out that Collins's previous book, *Built to Last: Successful Habits of Visionary Companies* (1994), did not address this subject. Rather, *Built to Last* focused on companies that were great from the start. Although *Good to Great* was written after *Built to Last,* Collins suggests that readers think of *Good to Great* as a prequel to his earlier book. This is because it offers readers a way to get to greatness in the first place, before they begin to think about the work of sustaining that greatness.

Thank you for purchasing this
Instaread book
Download the Instaread mobile app to get unlimited text & audio summaries of bestselling books.

Visit instaread.co
to learn more.

END OF INSTAREAD~~~~~~

References

[1] Spinner, Jeff. 1991. "Constructing Communities: Edmund Burke on Revolution". *Polity* 23 (3). Palgrave Macmillan Journals: 395–421. p.400.

[2] ibid., p.402.

42364563R00022

Made in the USA
San Bernardino, CA
01 December 2016